MW01591678

FAITHFULLY FINISHED

L. E. DAWSON

Copyright © 2019 L. E. Dawson.

All rights reserved. No part of this book may be reproduced, stored, or transmitted by any means—whether auditory, graphic, mechanical, or electronic—without written permission of the author, except in the case of brief excerpts used in critical articles and reviews. Unauthorized reproduction of any part of this work is illegal and is punishable by law.

Scripture taken from the King James Version of the Bible.

ISBN: 978-1-4834-9557-6 (sc)
ISBN: 978-1-4834-9559-0 (hc)
ISBN: 978-1-4834-9558-3 (e)

Library of Congress Control Number: 2018914915

Because of the dynamic nature of the Internet, any web addresses or links contained in this book may have changed since publication and may no longer be valid. The views expressed in this work are solely those of the author and do not necessarily reflect the views of the publisher, and the publisher hereby disclaims any responsibility for them.

Any people depicted in stock imagery provided by Getty Images are models, and such images are being used for illustrative purposes only. Certain stock imagery © Getty Images.

Lulu Publishing Services rev. date: 02/11/2019

CONTENTS

The only thing I've done to be worthy
Is plant a seed and decide to believe.

The only thing that makes me complete
Is the author of my faith who faithfully finishes me.

PREFACE

Life is not easy. It will give you moments that you wish would never end and moments where you wish you could press the fast-forward button. My journey is like a rainbow, yet the colors are not always so bright. The picture is not always clear. Life's rainbow, in its multitude of experiences, is beautiful, yet to really know its beauty, you must know its antagonist, pain. In the moments of fear, courage is born; through hopelessness, faith is renewed. Through dread, anticipation can move forward. The rainbow only gets its colors and radiance from the balance life provides.

This book of poems is my rainbow. These are my words of hope, fear, depression, love, and faith.

I pray that my testament will feed your rainbow.

Much love,

L. E. Dawson

WHY?

You might ask me, "Why do you write?"
The simple truth is I like to bring joy to life.
I like to share feelings as if they're my own,
Hoping to help people feel they're not alone.

It's also a type of therapy,
Processing emotions that are unclear to me,
Helping me find the path to clarity.

I also write because I didn't believe
That God would give this type of gift to me.
I shied away from it constantly,
Really just running from my destiny.

So today, I write this from my soul so deep:
Don't give up your dreams for anything.
Yes, you may have challenging situations you're going through.
That just means your story will be more beautiful.

HIS PLAN

My story is not over; as a matter of fact, it's just beginning.
This is a new chapter, and the last chapter is finally ending.
You would have thought I was in a drama, a mystery, maybe a horror show.
It was hard to see it is a story about resilience and hope.

All I know is that I'm entering the chapter where blessings flow,
Where I still will have trials and tribulations but I know who holds me close,
Where I still may have heartache and pain, but today is different; circumstances have changed.
What has changed is what I let inside me, whom I surround myself with, and who I choose to be.

I choose to be a survivor, a woman of truth, and a loving mother.
But beyond these things, I use faith as my cover.
It surrounds me; it's in me; it carries me.
It keeps me focused on those things I can't see,
Like God's amazing love for me.

I know he loves me, because I wouldn't be where I am today.
I would not have found this path; he wouldn't have let me know that I had gone astray.
He showed me a different path; he says, "It is yours to take."
So I took the first step, and he hasn't left yet.

So while my world is different, and I have much clarity,
I know there are still trials and tribulations waiting in the world for me.
But there are also joy and fulfillment and God's plan for me,
And having his plan tells me I can be what he wants me to be.

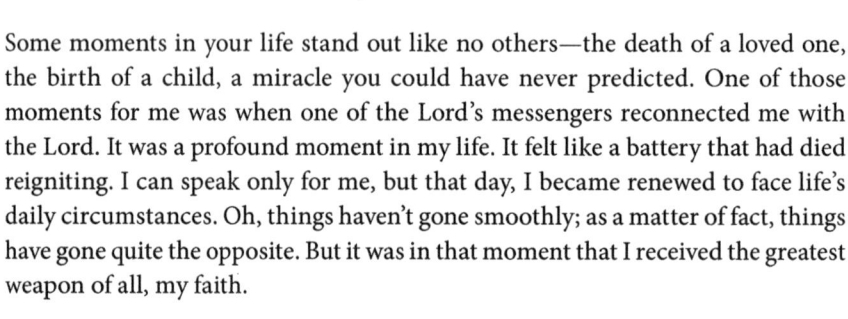

Some moments in your life stand out like no others—the death of a loved one, the birth of a child, a miracle you could have never predicted. One of those moments for me was when one of the Lord's messengers reconnected me with the Lord. It was a profound moment in my life. It felt like a battery that had died reigniting. I can speak only for me, but that day, I became renewed to face life's daily circumstances. Oh, things haven't gone smoothly; as a matter of fact, things have gone quite the opposite. But it was in that moment that I received the greatest weapon of all, my faith.

FROM DARKNESS TO LIGHT

The words flow from the depths of my soul,
Which thanks you from darkness, the light it beholds.
Deadened by starvation, calling a dark abyss its home,
Not really lonely with so many others around,
Buried by life with all its heartaches and pain,
No nourishing of my spirit, so complacent I became.

My starving spirit looked for food eventually.
Through his message that he gave you and that you poured into me,
Through the renewing of my spirit,
Through your faith and God's Word,
I gained a moment of clarity to step out with God's love.

Called by the Word that rings holy and true
Given to our spirit to nurture us through,
It's a light of purity; it's a light of love;
It's a relationship with our Father
That had been there all the time.

I needed a reintroduction, although he already knew me.
I know he looked at you and said, "Thank you for bringing my child
to me.
Every person you touch, every fire you ignite
Makes the angels sing praises for guiding spirits to my light."

5

Darkness can show up and bring many different things.
None of that matters, because God's light conquers everything.
Your words of conviction, with the Bible as your core,
Feed my faith and nurture my spirit with my relationship restored.

Your purpose is significant, a divine calling like no other,
Showing us a clear path to having a relationship with our Father.
So today, we say, "Thank you," to God for sending us you.
We pray for your spirit to always be renewed.
We pray for your family to always stay strong,
Building our faith and impact as a church family until God calls us home.

BELIEVE IN YOUR PURPOSE

It was God's gift to me.

It was my purpose, my destiny.

He gave it to me on my birthday, you see.

It was there the day I came into this world, the day I came to be.

He told me, "It is yours to give.

It's inside you; it's the place where I live.

Where your heart, spirit, and faith coincide,

It's in that place I reside.

When you opened up and let me in,

You gave a way for your talents to begin

To show up when you are walking your path."

When you build your relationship with God, you'll be shown all you have—

Not just all you have but all he has to give,

All the blessings and lessons when you walk with him.

It's amazing that it was there all this time,

That it was waiting for me to recognize what was mine.

So believe, believe, and believe some more.

You'll be amazed at what knocks at your door—

Destiny, purpose, impact, and a relationship that will last the test of time.

It's yours, so take it; don't leave it behind.

I had to learn that all who profess God's word don't actually know the author. This discernment grew in me rather quickly because I needed to understand God's word for myself. I could do so only if I built my personal relationship with the Lord. In that personal relationship, I learned to hear the Lord directly in my life, my situation, and my heart. God's Word doesn't need an interpreter. Yes, we can go to church to learn and grow, but the key thing I have to remember is that I must seek, I must learn, and I must trust and pray for wisdom.

You most definitely can gain wisdom through fellowship with others, through a spiritual mentor, and through a church family that is covered in God's grace. Those things matter, but in the end, what matters most is your relationship with the Lord. It is there and only there where your discernment will grow.

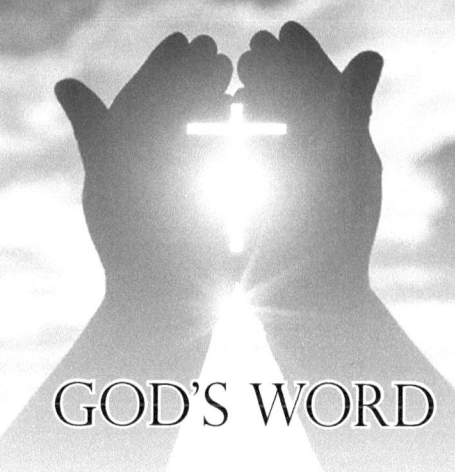

GOD'S WORD

Feed me.
While I'm full, I'm still fainting from thirst.
My appetite is sated, but my soul cries the worst
Because it hasn't been fed for many, many years.
I come here every Sunday, yet I find no nourishment here.

I thought this was supposed to be like an all-you-can-eat buffet,
Where I go with my church family so we can celebrate our faith,
Where I swallow God's Word because it's enough to fill my cup.
But when you cover it with foolishness and messiness, it makes me not
want to pick it up.

God's Word is not tainted.
It's the purest food you can eat.
You don't need to save it for special occasions.
You don't need sides to go with the meat.

God's Word is the main dish.
We choose to add the sides,
Where we start to lose focus on what he can do in our lives.

God's Word is everlasting.
It stretches from the beginning to the end.
It blankets me in his presence.
It forgives me for my sins.

God's Word is the truth.
It can't be twisted for gain.
It really has all the nutrients
That I need to maintain—

Not just to maintain my soul but to grow my faith tenfold.
It needs to fill me up until I overflow,
Because in that overflowing,
I have more of God to give—
Because through my abundance, they can see that God lives.

So I need to feed my soul each and every day.
I won't let it get thirsty, because that's when the devil will say,
"Why do you keep eating food that doesn't satisfy you?
I've got something better for you to chew.

Why do you keep returning time after time?
You might as well let that thing die.
Trust me; you'll be just fine.
Just feed your flesh until your time is up."

But my soul tells me I have more work to do.
God says, "Please know my Word; it has all the answers to pull you through.
My Word will give you everything to endure

This famine of destruction across the land,
The soulless ways that I see in your fellow man."
God says, "Don't worry; I have a plan."

So in his Word, I will stand,
And I will allow him to always hold my hand,

Because if he has it, I know he'll never let go.
I know this because his Word told me so.

So now, I believed, and in that belief, my superiority grew. I knew more, could share more, and felt confident I lived to help others.

The next poem makes me so happy because I wrote it at a point in time I forgot that I am still a pupil. While we are all teachers, we must remember we are students as well. Every day, I learn more. And to learn, you must stay grounded in the truth that you will always remain the student. My path is no different from anyone else's. My knowledge can prove helpful at times, and at other times, I am here to learn. For me, my humbleness grew here, along with the clarity that I am no better than anyone else. The only thing I have that we all have is mercy, which he freely gives.

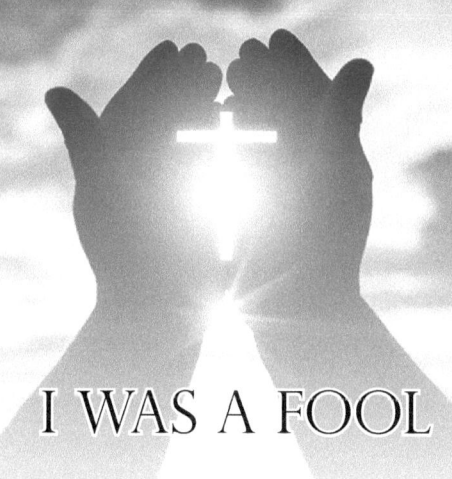

I WAS A FOOL

I was a fool because my body was broken.
I thought it took my soul, but I had misspoken.
I was a fool to put trust in man
When you told me all things are in your hands.
I was a fool to believe that it was already done.
Then you told me, "This battle has already been won."
I was a fool to rely on what I see,
'Cause through faith in those things unseen, all things can be achieved.
I was a fool who let my pain rule me,
But through your loving hands, you've schooled me.
You've taught me mercy, patience, and loving grace.
Now, I stand here with new bits of wisdom to shore up my faith.
I was a fool who's a fool no more;
Through faith and God, clarity is my reward.

RESTING

Extreme fatigue, I've been running for so long.
My soul and heart ache so much I'm having a hard time pressing on.
Running toward, running away, stopping to see where I'm at,
My tired spirit has had no place to rest.

This weariness is settling into my soul,
Weighing me down, slowing me 'cause it has caught hold.
I'm tired—I'm *so* tired. I just want to be,
Not weighed down so much with life's infirmities.

I've tried, I've tried so many avenues—
Praying for directions, searching every corner, looking for clues.
I'm exhausted. How do I know, God, if it's really you?
I want to do your will, but I just don't know what to do.

I can rest and not faint if I remember his provision.
He'll walk with me, carry me through every possible condition.
There's no weariness if I rest in the bosom of the Lord,
Holding my faith as my shield and the Word as my sword.

There's no burden, no situation that he can't carry me through.
Faith in him and him alone gives peace and renews.
I should be full and joyous of spirit in the midst of a storm
Knowing God holds my soul close and safe from harm,

For his yoke is easy and his burden light.

There's no need to be weighed down by the trials and tribulations in life,

For his Word remains true, never changing; what he says will come to be.

So, standing in his Word, resting in his arms, is where you'll find me.

STEP INTO THE FIRE

Step into the fire and feel the flames.
It burns away your grime and sinning ways.
It exposes what's buried underneath—
The hurt, rejection, pain, and defeat.
It engulfs those things that don't come from me,
Leaving you open and exposed to new ways of being.

In those new ways, new life can be born;
New purpose, new learnings with meaning can be formed.
No need to cry, feel lost, or mourn,
For in the fire, you can cast your sins,
Knowing that they can be judged to die, never to rise again.

Then I'll give to you a fire that will dwell in thee,
Helping you gain new knowledge and wisdom of me,
Helping you call out and cast all your cares on me,
Knowing that I hear you and I will never leave,

For my fire is a good thing and my burden light.
It can burn away hurt and rejection in your life,
For I want to always be there and dwell in thee.
I've wanted you since the beginning of time to be with me,

For with this fire, I give you the power to be
Victorious, walking in dominion, not believing defeat,
'Cause victory is ours, this battle has already been won.
It was finished that day by my begotten Son.
However, you're still on the battlefield, 'cause there's more work to be done.
There are more lives to be saved who don't know me.
There are people who don't know I am everything they need.

So, step into the fire and stay in the fire, praying day and night, and
I will continue to pour into you my flame of life.
It's not easy—I know it's not easy—but I know one thing for sure.
The fire will give your spirit the food it needs to endure—
Not just endure but mature to a whole new level,
Giving you faith and confidence to thwart the devil.

He wants you to believe that your pain, hurt, disappointments are the way you'll end,
That you'll stay in darkness, shying away because of your sins.
But in the flame come forgiveness and the burning light
That lets you shine and the world know you're a child of mine.

So, shine in the flames, shout, "Hallelujah!" and let the devil see
That those who step into the fire are now home with me.

MY EVENING PRAYER

Thank you, Lord, for letting me get through another day,
For blessing my family with trivial worries and relieving my spiritual worries.
Thank you for walking with me, loving me, and keeping me.
Thank you for the food that nourishes my body.
Thank you for the peace you have given me.
Thank you for the opportunity to serve you and grow in you.
I love you, and I'm in awe and can't comprehend your love for me.
And I thank you for residing in me so that I'm never alone.
Lord, I ask for purpose in you,
A spiritual feeding of serving you.
I ask that my spirit stands boldly before you, screaming, "Amen!" to the Lord I serve.
I pray for full confidence that I am walking in you.
I pray for a humble spirit that stays grounded in your ways.
I pray for a guiding vision to see what you would have me see.
I ask that your angels walk with me and help me sing your praises.
I want to be a muse for lost souls, inspiring them toward you,
Living in you.
When I lie down, I want to wake up renewed in you.
I pray for my life and that no evening is in vain,

No moment taken for granted.
Thank you, and I love you.
In Jesus's Magnificent name, I pray.

Amen.

GROWING UP AMONG
THE WEEDS

Sometimes, it's hard sharing space with weeds;
They clog my space, absorbing nutrients I need.
Growing faster and bigger every single day,
They look like they are prospering, having little hope or faith.

But the gardener sees and knows what is really growing;
Come harvest time, the weeds are left there, burning.
No matter how big they are, ashes are to what they're turning.
So, I need to stay in my place of prayer and enduring.

The weeds get the same sunshine to help them grow.
The weeds share the same soil, so they should know,
But they don't because they eat a different food.
Not knowledge and truth but lies are what they chew.
Sometimes, it's ignorance or doubt they hold on to.

If I don't hold on to truth and light, I just might believe
That I'll be choked and suffocated, swallowed up by the weeds.
The master gardener gives me grace and mercy.
It's the same opportunity the weeds get to have.
The only difference is I choose to grab it.

Weeds are still beautiful if you take a different view—
The view of the master gardener who can wash them anew.
It's not too late; it's not over, because they still have time—
Time to change before the harvest or else be left behind.

It's my place not to judge but only to pray—
Pray a prayer of thanksgiving for his mercy and grace,
Pray for the others who could be saved just like me.
If they shed their doubts, plant a seed of faith, and just believe—
For God gave us a seed that can grow and be multiplied—
With the nutrients from the Holy Spirit, they will help faith thrive.

Growing up among the weeds is not a bad thing.
It only amplifies the joy that God's presence brings.
The master gardener has a request that we tend the weeds.
He wants us to change lives, helping weeds become seeds,
For seeds multiply and can bear fruit,
Spreading his message of forgiveness, light, knowledge, and truth.
So, know you are planted where he wants you to be,
For the only way to do his work is to be next to the weeds.

LORD, THANK YOU

Lord, thank you for using me.
Thank you so much for your grace and mercy,
For I believe in you, Lord, more and more each and every day.
Thank you for never leaving me and helping grow my faith.
You are awesome, amazing, beautiful in your love for me.
You continue to reward my walking in faith and obedience.
In this moment, I shout, "Hallelujah!" praise God, bless his holy name.
I can't get over your love for me and my fellow man.
I sit here in awe and at peace, believing you cover me.
I sit here in awe of the gifts and purpose you have for me.
You shine upon my life this very day,
Lighting my path and slowly showing me your godly way.
I thank you; I thank you for never giving up on me,
Showing me my path through the things I can achieve.
Because of you, all things are possible in my life.
Because of you, I'll finally take back what's mine.
It was a gift from you so long ago,
One I recognize today as my very own.
Thank you, God; I praise your holy name.
In Jesus's name, I give thanks today.

YOUR CENTER

"My grace is sufficient for you, for my power is made perfect in weakness. Therefore, I will boast all the more gladly about my weaknesses so that Christ's power may rest on me. That is why, for Christ's sake, I delight in weaknesses, in insults, in hardships, in persecutions, in difficulties. For when I am weak, then I am strong." 2 Corinthians 12:9 King James Version

Your center is your weakness; that's where your strength lies.
It's when you let go and cry out to our God that your strength does arise,
For in your darkness and deepest despair, call out to God, and he is there.
You are not alone, never, for he cares for you and loves you so;
You may not hear or see him, but he always holds you close.

The winds may blow and sway you,
Making you feel like you are unsteady.
But in those moments, you are moving to where he is getting you ready.

Your life mate is your anchor whom God led you to,
For he is preparing you both for glory and the work he has for you.
So, lie down in your weakness, your situation, and your circumstance
Because when you lie down, you are resting in his mighty hands.

No need to wonder if you are lost and where you go from here.

No need to hold it together, because God knows what you fear.
Please rest with peace and give God your burdens.
Give him the confusion, the despair, and all those things that are hurting.

Then take a deep breath of relief and inhale his truth
That no person nor weapon will take away what he is preparing for you,

Because it is preparation, it's enhancement, not defeat,
For soon, you will turn a corner to find the generational curses lying at your feet.

BE A LEADER IN ME

My vision for the world is that they find me,
That we are reconciled for all eternity,
That their sins are forgiven if they trust in me,
That my promises will all come to be.

Because Satan didn't believe in that vision,
He tempted man to create a division,
Showed him knowledge that didn't come with wisdom
So that man could die without reconciliation.

But there is only one leader, and I'm in control.
All your trials and tribulations and your heart I know.
Each and every day, I watch your trust in me grow.
Each and every day, new wisdom unfolds.

I've given you a gift of mercy and grace.
I ask that you trust in me and keep the faith,
For out of faith birth goodness and knowledge of me.
With growing knowledge and self-control, you can achieve.
Self-control helps you conquer the desires of man—
Helps you persevere, endure, and continue to stand,
For then you are standing in my Word and my grace.
You are standing in the promises I have made to the human race.

Within those promises, you have built a heart to serve,
For you a leader now, 'cause you know your worth.
I sent a precious gift so that you could return to me.
I want you to share the good news with those who don't believe,
For your mission is to help others return to me.
Let them know the promises made to all who believe,
Sharing how my mercy and grace have allowed you to stand,
Sharing how I've always had a special love for man.

You were created in my image and my image alone.
I breathed into you spiritual life before you were born.
I wanted you to recognize who dwells in thee—
That I'm the truth, the light, the Father to all those who believe.

You were wonderfully and fearfully made.
You were given gifts, talents, and a purpose to share with the human race,
For in your serving and giving, you are a leader in me.
I will always provide every tool you ever need.

Know that I will give you the words, the abilities, and my message to share.
Know that your tears don't fall on deaf ears, 'cause I'm always there.
Know that you can stand with your head held up high
Because you are bathed in forgiveness with no condemnation in my eyes.
So, go forward with purpose, destiny, and grace.
So, go forward, sharing the good news about the author of your faith.
I will hold you and comfort you and always be there.
All you need to do is lay your burdens down in prayer.

Then hold fast because I will always take it from there.

TAKE MY HAND

Take my hand,
Hold it tight, and stay with me.
Never look down or backward; there's nothing there to see.

Wipe those tears from your eyes.
I am there with you,
Seeing what you don't see and how you will make it through.

Cease those words of condemnation and of self-doubt.
Speak of your mighty future and how you make it out.

Believe and walk in faith and trust the Lord,
For he is always faithful and sticks to his Word,
For he said he loves you and you will always be
A child whose Father is a King.

HIS PROMISES

Although I'm not where I want to be spiritually,
I know there are others taking their own journey with me,
Walking with God, learning his Word,
Finding the path that God has designed.

I fall sometimes in the temptation of sin.
It's hard to resist; I try not to give in,
Because I can glimpse what he sees in me.
When the clouds briefly clear,
I see the talents and beauty he has designed in me.

I want them to shine.
I want them to shout.
I want them to grow.
I want to bring them out.

I want the whole wide world to know
It's because of his goodness
That all my blessings flow.

You can have him as well; there's enough to go around.
He loves you too, just like me.
He's placed in you unique talents and beauty.

They're yours alone, not made for me.
They're designed for you; they're yours to see.

Take 1 percent of how much God believes in you;
It's enough to make sure that what you aspire to comes true.
Take 1 percent of God's faith in you.
You'd conquer the world; there's nothing you couldn't do.

Take 1 percent of God's love for you;
You'd weep with joy, feeling love so consuming.
Take 1 percent of God's forgiveness for you;
You'd make peace with everyone who has ever hurt you.

I took 1 percent faith, and it was enough for me to see
That God is God.
His Word is truth.
His promises will all come to be.

So, I know that if I fall, God will pick me up—
That he is enough to fill my cup.
If I slow down, he will keep pace;
He will be at the finish line when I am done with this race.

MIND

My mind is my best friend.
It's also the thing that tries to do me in.
When it's on, I feel that I can be all that I can be.
When it's not, I feel so defeated.
It keeps me there and says, "Let's sit until I have a plan;
I need to think about this situation I'm in."
Then God says, "Your mind won't figure it out.
If it could, defeat would have never come out."

I must renew my mind each and every day.
I must renew it in God, the author of my faith.
My mind alone will never be enough.
It's highly functioning and equipped with some powerful stuff.
It likes to suck in the things it sees.
Sadness and defeat are a powerful disease,
Making it physically hard to cope.

God says, "I have the cure for your mind disease.
It's not a pill or a class; it's trusting in me."
When you trust, you believe and you know
That God is with you, the protector of your soul.

He protects your soul, and your soul should lead your mind—
Not the other way around, else troubles you find.
Feed your soul so it's strong and it can be
The thing that constantly tells your mind to believe.

THIS MOMENT

Take a big breath, then sigh.
Close your eyes and listen because I'm right beside you.
Tell me what's wrong, what hurts, and all your fears.
I'm here; I'm listening; I'll wipe those tears.
There's nothing you can't overcome when you trust in me.
Just breathe and say, "I can do anything."
There's nothing you can't achieve when you stop and say,
"I need help. I need strength. Please, Lord, help me today."
I know it's tough; some days, it's hard to deal.
The things that can happen to you, in the moment, seem so surreal.
But in this moment, remember that you are not alone—
That I'm here and I've seen how this moment you've already overcome.

WAITING HERE FAITHFULLY

He has come for you to be forgiven of your sins,
For they were nailed to the cross to never rise again,
For you can release all that guilt, the pain and shame.
The Lord says they're not yours; you've got a new name,

For you've come out of the dark into the marvelous light,
For you're still fighting your flesh.
But the light makes it all right.
The road is so narrow, and it is long.
Your own strength you can't rely on,
For you will get weak; the shadows will return,
Your light so dim you can't go on.
Then you'll need to reach down into your soul so deep and cry out,
"Lord, please don't depart from me."

I know it gets hard; I can feel my own doubt.
I pray to you, Lord, that you lead me out.
Your Word is always true; what you say will come to be.
So, I will trust you, Lord, waiting here faithfully.

In times of stress, in times of doubt,
In times of illness, you'll lead me out.

Your Word is always true; what you say will come to be.
So, I will trust you, Lord, waiting here faithfully.

In times of pain, in times of loss,
In times of death, you've paid the cost.

Your Word is always true; what you say will come to be.
So, I will trust you, Lord, waiting here faithfully.

In times of debt, in times of chains,
In times of bondage, you've set us free.

Your Word is always true; what you say will come to be.
So, I will trust you, Lord, waiting here faithfully.

In times of hurt, in times of shame,
The Lord says you're free; you've got a new name.

Your Word is always true; what you say will come to be.
So, I will trust you, Lord, waiting here faithfully.

In times of sin where the flesh is strong,
The only weapon I call is a godly one.

Your Word is always true; what you say will come to be.
So, I will trust you, Lord, waiting here faithfully.

Does reading the news ever make a small part of you lose faith in the good of humanity? The world is a dark place; we can't deny that. Each day, we see acts that diminish our belief in each other. I think that we are wired to find those dark things. In many ways, it can be a selfish trait.

I must admit I have found myself feeling better once I have seen that I don't have it as bad as others. Of course, I feel guilty for saying that and even worse for putting it down on paper, but it's my truth. Then one day, a thought hit me: every bad situation gives hope an opportunity to show up. Without sadness, sorrow, worry, grief, fear, and a host of other depleting emotions, hope and faith could never show how much power they hold. Without hurt, we could never have healing. I found these thoughts profound.

I know that we always talk about yin and yang and the world needing balance, but I had never thought that hope cannot exist without its counterpart. So now, when a tough situation presents itself or when I experience the depleting feeling of sorrow, I plant a seed of hope and an expectation that the counterpart of whatever I feel will manifest itself in my life.

HOPE

Hope is lost.
It got caught up and tied down by sorrow, regret, and pain.
The new rules of the future make hope not want to appear again.
Where the news, violence, senseless acts, and hate bombard us every day,
It's hard to find hope wanting to mix in with the fray.

It could appear if we let it, but that means that we would have to let it in.
It would have to reside in us for hope to truly begin—
To be birthed into our nations, our societies, and our homes.
Hope doesn't want to live in a residence where it's all alone.

So, build it and plant it and allow it to grow.
Give it rich soil and fertilizer just to let it know
That you're here with hope for the long haul,
That you will resist the temptation of defeat when it calls.

Hope lets you see a better tomorrow.
Even though the vision could be murky and foggy,
It's still a direction for you to take
To start to leave your current circumstances in your wake.

If it's not hope for you, I could use some more, you see;
We all could use more hope in our society.

The benefits of hope outweigh its harm.
If you have no hope, you can't believe in anyone.

If there is hope, the world has more potential—
More possibilities, outcomes, and solutions to tap into.
It gives you a river to pull from,
A place to rest, and part of the spiritual nourishment that you need.
Hope can be a pretty powerful core rock indeed.

Don't take me at my word; try it on so that you can see
Hope is powerful and gives you a reason to believe.
I hope you hear me and will answer my call
To allow hope back in, which will benefit us all.

One day, I got in an argument with a loved one. It was a pretty intense argument where I said some hurtful things—things that I cringe at now when I think about them. At the time, I didn't know I was a writer. I knew that I best processed my thoughts by writing. I knew that sometimes, I felt great release with a piece of paper and a pen in front of me. I knew the power of words and how to state something in the most cutting way. My weapon was words, and they were always ready—always available—and I never ran out.

In the midst of this argument, I got up and I walked away. I learned such a valuable lesson that day. I let tears of frustration and anger fall, and I said a little prayer to help me write what I had in my heart. The following poem was born. It took me five minutes to write it, and once I wrote it, I began to cry in earnest. My poem wasn't about my anger, the fight I had just had, or my frustration. It spoke into existence what I knew to be true but had forgotten for a minute—that we wrestle with things unseen, and that the devil will make the pain of a scratch into a festering wound if we allow it.

I hadn't realized what was happening in that moment until I read my poem. As a matter of fact, what we were arguing about was so stupid that I found it hard to comprehend my level of anger associated with the argument. As soon as I reabsorbed the words on paper into my being, a burden disappeared, and I laughed. The person I was arguing with heard my laughter and came into the room to see what was so funny after this major fight. I looked at them and said, "I love you." Guess what? They didn't expect to hear these words; these words flabbergasted—confused—them, and I saw peace descend upon them. These words released both of us to return to who we were supposed to be. Whatever had existed in that room during the fight left because we no longer invited it in.

FILLED

My soul is claimed, and you can't have it.

My sons are claimed, and you can't have them.

Devil, I see what you are trying to do, and guess what? God sees it too.

I plead the blood of Jesus over my family.

I plead the blood of Jesus over my husband.

I plead the blood of Jesus on everything you have tried to take.

I give you your anger back; I give you your hate back; I give you your darkness back.

I'm filled with Jesus; there's no room for you.

I'm filled with hope; there's no room for despair.

I'm filled with love; there's no room for hate.

I'm filled with truth; you can take your lies.

I'm filled with faith, especially now, since you showed up.

Why me; why now? Because God loves me; that's why.

What he loves, you can't take.

What he's claimed, you can't claim.

Where I'm going, you can't go.

Where I am, you can't be

Even if you try to share the same space with me,

For I am covered in his blood and in his name.

My Heavenly Father has me.

I've made plenty of mistakes. If I had a penny for every mistake I've made, I would be the richest person on the planet. When I think about some of my mistakes, it amazes me how much I've recovered from them. I look back and think, *Who was that person, and why the heck did she do what she did?*

Previously, even when I felt happy about my progress, I still had things in life that I had yet to fix or complete. I looked at my past and had immense regrets. The reality is nothing in your past can fix your future. So, finally, I had to train myself to stop looking back and to focus on what lies ahead.

FUTURE

What happens if you leave your future in your past?
Will you always turn around, looking for the things that are out of your grasp?

Will you always replay what has already gone?
Will you walk backward instead of moving on?

Will you long for things long gone by?
Will you cry and wish you could go back in your life?

Time waits for no one,
Including your past.
Time truly knows that what's current won't last—
That your moments are not behind you but waiting for you to grasp.

Time knows that the future is always a step ahead.
It's hard to catch up if you're looking backward instead.

So, keep moving with anticipation of what's to come—
A brighter future of possibilities that have just begun.

You can't fight a war alone,
Unless it's just yourself you're fighting with.

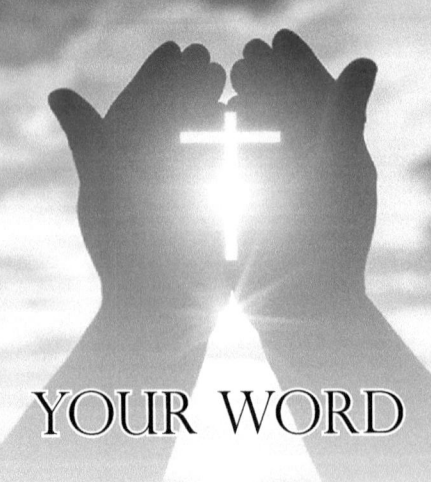

YOUR WORD

"Your word is your bond."
I wonder if that's true you.
Do you always follow through on everything you say you'll do?

Or are your words fleeting
And given out like candy?
You're sort of like a mechanic; you use them as tools when they're handy.

What happens when you use them for the wrong purposes?
Then you come to find in the future your word is worthless.
It's like currency no one wants to use, because in the past, your word was abused.

It might have changed with no notice, or maybe there was no follow-through.
You might've given your word with your mouth but your head said, "No, we won't do
Whatever it is you're committing to."

Your word is a diamond only if you execute.
It becomes a cheap trinket if you don't do what you said you would do.
That's when mistrust, doubt, skepticism, and regrets will follow you.

Breaking your word will destroy many bonds over time
Because no one wants to deal with an unreliable liar.
Your word is a currency, more valuable than money,
So, carry your word close, and give it out sparingly.

Hold on tight to your word, your God-given wealth,
And always, with your word, remain true to yourself.

Faith is a journey, one that has moments where you can feel so close to the Lord and other moments where darkness surrounds you. I remember the first moment that I fell in love with God. I felt euphoric in my joy. Every distress that I had in my life seemed small because I knew that God walked with me. I prayed faithfully, read the Bible daily, and sang constantly with a joyful spirit.

I remember sitting at home reading a daily devotional; I had one sent to me every morning. This one was called "When We Fell in Love." It talked about how you should do those things that you did when you first fell in love with the Lord, when you shared your newfound relationship and everyone could see the joy that you held in your heart. It talked about remembering those moments because time makes memories of previous revelations and joy, like many things in life, fade. When I read this devotional, I really couldnis devotionalhose moments becauseyour heart. I found it too precious, and I had never felt such peace before.

Today, I look back and feel sad because I never saw the signs. For example, maybe I skipped a devotional because I became busy and had to leave early for work. Perhaps I skipped it because I had to cook dinner and I fell asleep afterward because I was so tired. All of a sudden, those small changes led me to not make daily time with the Lord. Then I found that those moments turned into days and days turned into weeks. I felt embarrassed and then ashamed at how fickle I became. In my shame, I questioned how I could go back to spending time with God when he knew how much I lacked devotion.

Then one day, in my emptiness, I said softly, "Lord, I'm here." Deep in my soul, I heard the answer back, saying, "I'm always here." I began to cry—cry with loneliness that I had missed out on my relationship and my connection due to shame. I asked for forgiveness and asked, "Can I start over?" The response had no hesitation, only love and acceptance.

I still fight those feelings of inadequacy and fickle demonstration of my faith. Now, I know that those are just lies to keep me from returning to my strength, my confidence, my hope, and so much more. The Lord placed in my heart a belief that every day, I can rediscover him, and he is never lost or gone; as long as I have breath, I can inhale his presence into my life. Every day is a new day to rediscover, learn from, and grow in the Lord. Every day is a new day to feel God's love. Every day is a new revelation with new insight, new knowledge, and an opportunity to grow my relationship and faith.

MY CONFESSION

I have a confession I really must share.
While I have dreams, I'm scared my life is going nowhere.
While I have hopes, I have more doubts and fears.
While I have love, I let apathy enter my heart for those I hold dear.

While I have courage, I sometimes shy away
From the challenges that enter my life constantly.

While I have truth, I get caught up in lies.
I see with my unclear eyes.
I feel with my broken heart.
I walk this journey with my cracked feet.
Sometimes, I don't walk and choose to crawl.
The burdens of life make me want to give up on it all.

Then a voice reaches down and says,
"You don't have to do this alone; there's a different way.
Believe in hope and love; more important, continue to have a seed of
faith.
I hear you, I see you, I feel you, I know you, and I love you always.
You are special, unique, and a treasure to me.
I've counted the hairs on your head, and your tears I keep.

I keep them because everything about you is precious to me.

They'll be used to fertilize your path on this journey.
Your fear will become food to shore up your faith.
Your apathy will become nourishing love to lead the way.
Your broken heart will be mended; then you'll see
It was just put back together so you could love more fiercely.
Your challenges were stepping-stones so that you could see
That you were made to overcome anything.

Your unclear eyes were blurry only to you,
For I clearly see you and all the things you were made to do.
Just trust and believe in this one thing:
That I'm yours and you're mine and I'm not going anywhere.
I helped to pen this for this moment so that you know that I'm here.

What feels like a rope today will become your necklace,
Beautiful, shiny, and oh so precious."

"When I'm better." That was my answer; I would talk to God when I was a better person. I would share my relationship with God once I seemed worthy. I would go to church once I cleaned up my life.

I've learned that "When I'm better" is just a trap that says to wait until you feel worthy. But guess what? If you believe you aren't worthy in the first place and there is nothing that you can do on your own to become worthy, then you are waiting for a day that will never come. So, I turned my thinking around. Now, I think, *I'm perfect in my imperfection. I'm perfectly imperfect, which is the greatest thing I can offer.* I believe that I can be made whole only through my belief and faith in the Lord.

MESS

Why do you think God is not in your mess?
Mess for some is often a treasure for others.
Even with your faults, God loves you.

So, pick up your mess, your doubts and fears.
Drop them off at the altar, and leave them there.
It'll get sorted out, what you keep and what you toss.
God will figure it out; nothing will get lost.

Bring the whole bag, leaving nothing behind.
The master recycler will sort it out in time.

MORNING ROUTINE

I get up every morning and make coffee.
I add two spoons of sugar and cream.
Then I thought about my morning routine.
It's what I do each morning faithfully;
Even my dog could do it blindly.

I needed to create the right routine,
Thanking God each morning for blessing me—
For waking me up to continue to breathe,
For starting me on my way to experiencing new things,
For the two spoons of cream and sugar in my cup,
For the mug of coffee to lift me up.

Okay, after all, I'm human, but I need to remember and know
It's not from this cup of coffee my blessings flow.

MY COLLECTION

One day, I realized I was collecting pennies,
Never evaluating their worth, but boy, did I have many.

Then a friend said, "Why are you not picking up the gold,
The valuable nuggets that you hold?
You seem like you're frantic, picking pennies.
Yet if you stopped to pick up the gold, you'd have many;
Many more insights, lessons, growths would be your bounty.
Instead, you're counting the hill, not the mountain?"

I guess what I valued was easy to see,
Yet life lessons seemed too much of a burden to evaluate their quality.
Those lessons seemed to come at such a cost.
I guess I valued never what I gained but what I lost.

If I take the time to collect one ounce of gold,
It's worth a thousand pennies that I hold.
It takes reflection and time to understand its worth,
So, throughout my life, I'm going to put collecting wisdom, not knowledge, first.

SONG IN MY HEART
(KEEP HOLDING)

Keep holding God's hand.
Keep praying to him.
Keep him in your soul, and he'll hold you close.

Keep faithful and see
In him you can be
Everything that he sees, every possibility.

His Word is faithful.
His love remains true.
Don't ever
Stop chasing.
God is chasing you.

"Have a little talk with Jesus. Tell him all about our troubles." That is one of my favorite songs. While I love this song, sometimes, I look for other ways to make it all right. I may talk to my friends, my husband, my pastor, my mom, my dad, and even my dog, but I still feel a sense of discontentment. While they can listen and give me advice, they do not give me the counsel or rest I really seek.

I sometimes say to myself, *Yes, Lord, I know that you are there, but I really need someone I can physically hear right now.* Those thoughts that the Lord is not there and I need to hear directly from someone take me away from my greatest source. I find when I do turn to the Lord, I deeply feel that everything will be okay. While I can't hear him with my physical ears, the Lord creates other ways for me to directly hear what I need to hear. Sometimes, my spirit tells me insights I would have never gained, or the Lord places someone in my life and we have what I know is a divinely created interaction. In the end, I have learned that I need to start with the beginning. The Lord is my beginning; by starting there, I always end up where I need to go.

SOME DAYS

Some days, I feel down and wonder what's bothering me now.
It's really just a feeling and not one single incident.
I feel sort of unbalanced, not sick or unhappy,
A little off, like something doesn't make sense to me.

Those are the times I run to my quiet place
Just to sit down and reflect.
Then a peace takes over me.
A voice says so quietly,
"I'm glad you stopped for some time.
I missed you coming by.
I was hoping that you would hear me
And would want to spend some time being near me.

I just want a moment to check in and see how you've been.
Although I already know, hearing directly from you means more."

It's in that moment that my soul feels love overflowing.
It's not born from me but supplied graciously.

It's amazing that God seeks my attention.

I guess I shouldn't be surprised; God's been doing it all my life.

MUSING OF THE SOUL

Hope, which leads us forward
Love that always renews
Faith, which feeds our spirit
Truth that always endures

Joyful laughter, the balm to our soul
Peace, a place that lives within
God, a healer of many
The light that washes away our sins

Confidence in the valley
In darkness, guidance from our inner light
In temptation, courage to withhold from desire
In weakness, finding strength to endure this life

In all things, pray for directions.
Knock on the door
Seek and discover
What you need and so much more.

UPSET STOMACH

So, I ate something that made my stomach ache.
Whatever it was made me throw up right away.
I find it interesting that my stomach would reject bad food.
I sort of wish my brain had that reflex too.

It seems like my stomach was more advanced at times than my brain.
It knew that some things weren't very nourishing.
So, take a lesson from your stomach on what you give your brain as food.
Know that not everything you choose to absorb is meant for you.

SOMETIMES

Sometimes, I don't know how to control my pain.
My doubts, my fears, or my uncertainties,
They seem to take on a life of their own and overwhelm me.
They seem so significant in my current circumstance.
They make hope feel like it hardly has a chance.
But remember, that's when faith comes in to help you cope and believe;
Faith is the substance of things unseen.

Pain can become peace.
Doubt becomes confidence.
Fear becomes courage.
Despair becomes hope.

Faith, in its purest form, is just a seed.
The seed, if never planted, won't grow into a tree.
The tree, when nourished, will establish deep roots,
Making your faith the cornerstone of what you cling to.

YOUR STORY

What happens when your story is not the one you envisioned?
It's turning out to feel sort of like a crash-course collision
Of heartaches, sadness, disappointments, and pain.
As each page turns, you never want to revisit them again.

Don't always judge a book by its cover.
Don't get wrapped up in the current chapter, believing there're no others.
Don't believe that the ink is set in stone.
Believe that with each chapter, it gets better as you go.

Believe that you can author and change your own genre.
It still can be a story of triumph, of hope or resilience and not a drama.
It can be a story of strength, perseverance, and realized faith.
It can be a story of determination to change the next page.
Know that they're blank pages and it can be up to you
What you decide to turn those blank pages into.

PEACE

Today, I decided I wanted to live with peace.
That means we can't reside in the same house,
So today, I'm kicking you out.
You've been living here for too long.
I didn't realize that my joy had gone
Until I said, "Peace, please come back home.
I'm kicking sorrow and worry out so we can live alone.

When you were here, I was so happy.
I didn't let the little or big things bother me.
I remember when we would sit quietly, just happy to be together.
We used to go for walks, no matter the type of weather,
Through the storms that always raged in our lives.
It was always faith that got us by.
So, peace, I acknowledge that I let you leave.
Please forgive me; I'm ready for you to come back home to me."

DIVINELY CREATED

What makes up the body?
It's the sum of all its parts.
It's pieces put together, coupled with soul and especially the heart.
Every part of you serves a purpose.
Every part has a special design,
Every flaw uniquely yours,
Created by the Divine.

What was divinely fabricated
Was produced with loving hands.
If you feel like part of you is a mistake,
Remember that's the evaluation of man.

Every part of you is precious.
When you look through loving eyes,
You may not be able to see with your own,
But give God's eyes a try.

I know that seems impossible and hard to conceive.
Pray to God and ask, "Help me believe I am what you see."

YESTERDAY

I heard yesterday was rough
And not really what you expected.
Some people started to frustrate you,
Had you feeling sort of rejected.

Well, today, you face a dilemma:
Do you leave yesterday behind,
Or do you carry yesterday forward,
Keeping those things that happened fresh in your mind?

It really is a dilemma, because if you let go, what do they learn?
If you move on, what are the consequences for their creating all this churn?
Maybe the consequence of the situation is your choosing peace,
Being convicted that those things won't bother me.

It doesn't mean you're foolish and create a revolving door.
It just means you're more discerning of whom you open it for.

MY MORNING ANTHEM

I choose to float.
I don't want to settle.
I'd like to be the person who keeps her head up,

Looking in the direction of my goals,
Fighting the things that try to draw me down, blow by blow.
Relentless determination is my food.
Fortitude is my medicine to follow through,
Pushing past the things that stand in my way,
Climbing over my challenges,

Walking over my doubts one step at a time,
Getting back up when I'm knocked down,
Standing strong when the wind blows,
Knowing that I must keep going.

Progress is not made standing still.
Wishing is not the same as applying your will.
Desire is just what's in the mind.
I choose exertion coupled with belief that my goals can be realized.

A YEAR

It's amazing what can happen in a year.
A year ago, I lived in so much fear.
I didn't know how I could live.

A year ago, you found me with no hope.
A year ago, I barely knew how to cope.
A year ago, I was in so much pain.
A year ago, I was learning to live again.

A year ago, I was brought to my knees.
I learned how to beg and how to plead.
With the forces that surrounded my life,
I just didn't know how I would get by.

In those moments, I couldn't see.
I felt like I was stuck in my current circumstance permanently.

But just like winter, spring, summer, and fall,
Seasons change and evolve.
The cold and sparseness of winter will eventually
Birth the dew and flowers of spring's beauty.

Today, I write this in perspective as one year goes by.
I can finally look back and truly see
That a year ago was my foundation, preparing me for victory.

I WILL FOLLOW YOU

I will follow you, no matter the cost.
I will follow you, no matter what I lost.
Your treasures unmeasured, the depths of my soul,
Your glory I can't find if I shall not go.

Oh, I will follow you.

I will always seek your counsel every day.
I will always ask you to show me the way,
'Cause I don't want to use my eyes that cannot see.
I don't want to walk this path without you next to me.

Oh, I will follow you.

I will follow you on the narrow road.
I will follow you 'cause you've taken my load.
My burdens you've shared; I've laid them down in prayer.
You've always been my comforter; you've always been there.

Oh, I will follow you.

I will follow you; the passage is free.
I will follow you 'cause your Son paid for me.
One day, he died and gave me life;
He took my hand and brought me to the light.

I will follow you.

As I celebrated Easter, I wrote the following poems to reflect on those moments.

HIS DEATH

His death was life eternal
And forgiveness for our sins.
He died so that we could be with God again.
Jesus went to Jerusalem and suffered many things;
He lost his human life so spiritual life he could bring,
For we are God's, and he didn't want to see us die in sin.
So, he gave us the ultimate sacrifice so that we would be forgiven.
So, when Passover was two days away, Jesus predicted he would be crucified.
While the spirit was willing, Jesus's flesh was weak.
He prayed to God to take this cup from me.
Then Jesus taught us another important lesson that day:
Whenever we are weak, we should pray to God for strength,
For Jesus committed his spirit into God's hand.
He walked in his purpose and gave his life for man.
He breathed his last breath, and the Lord's will was done.
At that moment, it was finished so that we could be as one.

THREE DAYS

I could only imagine what the disciples felt those three days.
Judas took his life because his sin was truly great.
Peter denied Jesus as he gave his very life.
I'm sure that betrayal weighed heavy on his mind.
Jesus had died; his body hung from the cross.
Many thought the battle was over and the war for our soul was truly lost.
Those who knew him, including the women who had followed him from
Galilee, stood at a distance, watching these things.
Those three days when hope had left the world
Brought darkness and despair to our very soul,
For the son of man was gone, lying in a tomb.
Little did we understand he was preparing a way to be reborn.

HE ROSE

On the first day of the week, the women took the spices they had prepared.
They were surprised to find that Jesus wasn't there,
That he had risen, because this was a place for the dead.
Remember he told them he would rise again.
The woman told the men that he had risen.
They didn't believe the woman 'cause it sounded like nonsense,
But Peter, who denied him, ran to the tomb.
Seeing the strips of linen, he pondered what had happened,
For Jesus was gone from the place where he had been laid to rest.
On the road to Emmaus, Jesus appeared to two,
Who recapped to him what Jesus had been through.
Little did they know that the Messiah had risen again
Until they broke bread; it was then revealed to them,
For it was written in the law of Moses told by prophets and the Psalms
That the Messiah would suffer and die for our sins.
Once God's Word was fulfilled, we would be forgiven.

ALL PRAISE

So today, we celebrate and remember what God had done,
Sending us the ultimate sacrifice, his only begotten Son.
Rejoice; rejoice and remember that this is good news.
Remember Jesus's suffering and all that he went through,
Because when he died on the cross, he was thinking of you—
Yes, you and me and all of humanity.
He died and rose so that we might live again.

So, give thanks and praise to the one who loves us so.
So, give thanks and praise to the one who holds us close.
So, give thanks and praise for his love and grace.
So, give thanks and praise because our Redeemer lives today,
For this isn't history; it's our present where God is alive.
Look around the room because he lives in you and I.
So, all praise to our Redeemer, our God, for sending his Son,
For going to prepare a place for us so that we can be as one.

WHAT IF

What if I lived like today was my last?
Would it change whom I spoke to?
Would it change what I did?
Would it change anything about the last day I had to live?

Would I look at the sky differently?
Would I cherish what I had?
Would I kiss my loved ones, knowing tomorrow, they are out of my grasp?

Would I look back proudly, reminiscing over the things that I've done?
Would I feel contentment, knowing I've accomplished so much?
Would I feel peace in spirit, knowing I was kind to others?
Would I forgive those who hurt me and let go of any grudges?

If today were my last, it would put in perspective so many things,
Loving, seeking, forgiving, nourishing, and cherishing all that life brings.

HUNGRY

My stomach grumbled 'cause I was so hungry.
Then I thought about what type of food would be appealing to me.
I'm starving for a world with no hate.
I'm hungry for love to outweigh apathy.
I have a taste for outrage to break complacency.
I want the recipe to create income equality.
I want to savor children not being scared to sleep at night.
I want to smell what world peace would be like.
I want to sip on hope replacing fear.
I want to feel the fullness of a world with no one hungry.
I thought about the type of food that would satisfy me,
Wondering whom I could ask to cook the things I wished to see.
I realized it would take the whole world to create this recipe.
Please, will you come and cook with me?

LOVE LETTER

I love you.
Those are the only words that closely describe what I feel.

You're beautiful and smart, and your capabilities are surreal.
I want to see you live your life with abundance,
Believing that you can overcome anything—
All the roadblocks and frustrations that life will bring you.

Your intuition is spot-on and your humor all your own.
Each day you get stronger and smarter, the further along you go.

No looking back—only look forward, 'cause that's where you're going.
No need to worry, because you have a confidence that's all-knowing.
Yes, you'll make mistakes, but that's okay, because you will come back
With new knowledge and understanding, headed on the right path.

Each day, it becomes a little clearer and molded with sharper form,
Giving you shape and definition that's really hard to clone.
I love you, love you, love you, and I can always be there,
Buried down deep, keeping you steady, sort of like your anchor.
Holding me close means that you're always loved,
Always cherished and assured that you can conquer all.

Forever yours,
Self-Love

FOR YOU

I wrote this especially for you.
I see your kind spirit and all the turmoil you're going through.
Don't worry; God sees it too,
And I know he wants me to tell you he is there with you.

Your world has shifted, and things have changed.
Your future's unknown, but that is the same as yesterday.
Yet one thing is certain and remains the same:
You know who you are, and you know your name.

Know that this will not overtake you, only allow you to rise
Above the situation and circumstance
And prove to you that you're resting in God's hands.

He sees you, he knows, and he holds you close.
More important, he knows what you don't know.
He sees the outcome of all you're going through.
Just call on his strength, and he's there for you.

I know we don't always understand the why,
The reason, the cause for things that impact our lives.

Life is unfair, unjust in many ways.
It will throw curveballs to try to take away your faith.
In the end, the only thing this will do
Is show you God's glory and what he has for you.

TAKE THE WHEEL

Jesus, take the wheel because I can't drive.
I keep running into the wrong situations in my life.
I've decided I don't qualify for me to take the wheel,
So I'll just ask you to drive and hold still.

YEARNING

I yearn for something more in my life.
Each day that passes, I feel like I'm letting life die.
Chances are gone, and opportunities lie dormant.
My soul cries out, but I find ways to numb it.

Still in numbness, the crux of my situation is clear:
If I don't make any effort, I'll be forever stuck here,
Maybe not forever but more like the rest of my life.

If I don't create a plan, life is going to pass me by.
If I don't take steps, then I'll be stuck in this place.
If I don't start now, then I'll have wasted another day.

Then the days turn into weeks, into months, and I'm still here,
Frozen in time that didn't stand still, meaning I'm now in arrears.

I've missed life chances, leaving opportunities on the table.
If I'm still here, then there's a chance and I'm still able

To move forward, to see ahead, to hope and believe
That I can still change and design my future; it's really up to me.

MY WORTH

What is my worth?
Is it what I see reflected in my eyes,
Or is it what I accomplish in life?
Can my worth be articulated in deeds,
Or is it just reflected in earthly things?
Is my worth multiplied by my confidence?
Is it increased by my common sense?
Is my worth what you give to me,
Or is my worth calculated by what I take?
Is my worth the same as my value?
There's only one of me, which would make me indispensable.
If I'm replaced, does it degrade what I am?
Does it make me unworthy or less than?
Worth is a concept and nothing more.
It's how we measure what's important.
It changes with each new idea
Of what makes us feel more or less valuable.

I'm glad that God's worth for me never changes.
The way he loves me is absolute and the same
As today, tomorrow, and yesterday.

It doesn't change, no matter how much I fail or achieve.
So my worth is what he sees in me,
A precious child of the Almighty Being.
So who am I to judge for the King?

VOICE

I was looking for my voice, but then I realized it was never lost.
I was waiting for permission when, in reality, I was already granted admission.
It was my belief that was holding me back,
Stopping me from engaging, thinking that somehow my voice lacked
Authority, wisdom, knowledge, credibility, and know-how.
When, after all this time, I found that what I was allowing
Had kept me from being part of the conversation,
Thinking that I hadn't earned the right for participation,
Then I thought, *What would I do if I believed*
That my voice carried messages for change,
That my input was powerful, that it could change life outcomes?
Would it change how I choose to engage?
Would I step forward and fill out my space?
Would I take my seat at the table,
Or would I allow that vacancy to continue?
In the end, we all have lost
If we give up our right to share our voice.

THINKING OF YOU

I don't know the ways or the why.
I have no comprehension of the pain that resides in the tears you cry.
I don't know what it takes to fight this dark time,
Or the hopes and wishes you try to set aside.

All I know is that I pray for you.
I pray for the Lord's comforting presence to reside with you.
I pray that your tears are caught in his hand—
That you can draw on his strength and continue to stand.

I pray that through it all, you continue to hear
God's voice of love as it draws you nearer.
I pray that with each breath, your burden becomes lighter—
That in each exhale, your spirit receives fire;

That your inner light burns with spiritual intensity;
That it helps you cope in this darkest valley.
I pray with hope and faith and ask for all the Lord's mercy and grace
To help you continue to press on to survive whatever you face.

In Jesus's name, I lift you up in prayer.
I pray in every hard moment God meets you there.

MY SEASON

Lord, is it my season to walk in my wealth,
To have the beauty of my faithfulness felt,
To see your promises come alive in my life,
To see the darkness retreat, letting the light shine bright?

Is it my time to know your desires for me—
Not just know them but have them manifest in my reality?
I'm a little uncomfortable; I don't know what to do when you bless me.
I feel ashamed at my apprehensiveness, so unworthy.

You told me that the faithful shall see,
That your love is everlasting, and to hold on to my dreams.
You told me that your answer is always right on time,
That you will always carry me, and that with you by my side, I'll be fine.

I remember one night, in my despair, you told me what was waiting for me.
I held on to that moment, with my malnourished seed of hope, so desperately.

Then today, I realized your truth:
That my seed had grown with nourishment from you.
So today, I thank you for planting that seed in my life,

For giving me encouragement that your love will get me through the night.
Thanks for showing me that, after nightfall, there is always a brighter day;

That I will always be standing if I fall on my knees and pray;
That when I submit, I am oh so strong,
Because it's in that submission I allow my faith to lead me on
Directly to you as the center of my world.
You hold me steady, keep me anchored, and accelerate me to my purpose.

Lord, I love you, and I'm humbled that you chose me first—
That through you, I've finally realized my worth.

THANKFUL

What am I thankful for?
I'm thankful for the ability to be
Black, a woman, a mother, a Christian in this country.
I'm thankful for my extended tree, a complex multitude of family.

I'm thankful that I live in an era of hope
Where seeds of truth get planted and start to grow.
I'm thankful that darkness comes to light,
That our blemishes don't get the right to hide in the dead of night.

To put it quite simply, I'm thankful to be thankful.
No matter the cards of life, I've been giving my handful.
I'm thankful that I still have cards to play,
That I still get to choose on my life's journey.

THE TREASURE OF BELIEF

My light is something that can always be renewed.

I find my light is medicine to other people's issues,
Giving darkness, depression, sadness something to grab on to.

Giving it away makes it shine brighter—
Makes the burden of this world feel a little lighter.
The more I give it away, the more I feel renewed.
The more I let it go, I find something new to hold on to,

Which is my faith—that we are all someone's light,
Someone's beacon of hope in the dark, cold night.
Learning to give is learning to receive,
For in your giving, you walk in belief.

The gift of belief is a sacred treasure,
For it is in your belief that you can travel farther than you could ever
imagine.

BESIDE YOU

I wished upon a star.
It's not what I need—
The light of love to shine upon me.

I blew out the candle
In hopes that it would come true.
My desire is to be closer to you.

I found a four-leaf clover
And held it in my hand
And closed my eyes in hopes that I'd see love again.

No what matter what I do,
No matter how I dream,
I feel so alone, lost in society.

Your love feels far away,
Too distant to touch.
The absence leaves me cold,
My soul in a rut.

My prayers sometimes feel empty,
The conversations one-sided.
When you were talking to me, my attention was divided.

You brushed my cheek and said,
"I never let you go.
I desired your attention so that I could let you know

My love is ever faithful;
My commitment remains unwavered.
Through your fleshy eyes, you can't see I'm working in your favor.

You don't need any luck.
No charm works with me.
I told you that you were mine if you just believe.

Your burdens you can carry, or you can hand them to me.
The weight of your world was never yours to keep.

The silence that you hear
Is not because I'm not there.
I'm listening to your heart and what you say in prayer.

Don't ever feel alone; but if you do,
Remember my Word and my promises to you.
No matter the circumstances, my commitment is absolute.
I'll always be here right beside you.
I'll always be here right beside you.
I'll always be here right beside you."

BELIEVE

I believe in miracles.
Things that the eyes would never see
Come knocking on the door unexpectedly.

I believe in faith
In dark times, clinging to the withered thread,
Believing there's a path out of the circumstance.

I believe in hope,
Choosing to unfriend doubt,
Clinging to substances of love, trust, and faith that it will all work out.

I believe that love is a vital food,
One that you must constantly absorb to continue to press through.

Finally, I just believe
Without belief, faith, love, and hope can't mean anything.

RECONCILIATION

Our God is not one who divides; if anything,
He's the reconciliation coach in our lives
Helping us let go of broken things,
Coming full circle, guiding us through our pain,

Leading us out of darkness and away from fears,
Guiding us to his amazing light so that we can live,
Training our eyes to focus on the prize—
Not all the noise, churn, disappointments in our lives.

Reconciliation is about having to make it through.
It's in the reconciliation that we are born anew.

I COME TO YOU

I come to you for healing and understanding.
I come to you to be renewed.
I come to you to help see me through.
I come to you to praise your name.
I come to you because I have changed.
I start with you because you are the beginning and the end.
I start with the forgiver of my sins.
I start with you because you knew me first.
You were always there prior to my birth.
I start with you 'cause you showed me my worth.
You told me to lean on the Lord,
That my burdens are not mine alone,
That my sickness is not mine to own,
That my hopelessness has to go,
Because your loving arms hold me close.

ALL THINGS

God can do all things.

He can be your light in the darkness.
He can erase all your sorrow.
He can wash away all your sins
So that you can be with him.

He can be the light when you can't see,
The truth when there's make-believe.
He can bring you peace in the midst of war
'Cause he resides with us, our Lord.

He will be your food when you're hungry,
Water when you're thirsty.
He will always be with us, our Lord,
Our relationship restored.

No matter how we're lost,
Our God will lead us there
Out of our circumstance.
With him, we have a chance.

No matter how we're thirsty,
Trust in God, and all things come to be,
For in his Word, you'll stand,
'Cause he always has your hand.

No matter how you're sad,
Trust in God, and you will see
That you are never alone.
With him, you have a home.

FREEDOM

You have the freedom to forgive.
You have the right to love and let live.

You have the access to pray every day.
You have the choice to let go of hurts and walk away.

You have the right to hope for better things.
You have the grace and mercy that God brings.

You have the will and determination to live in victory.
You have a greater purpose and destiny than what the eyes can see.

You have wisdom waiting that's meant just for you.
You have fears and doubts that you're holding on to.

You have the freedom to believe the impossible and dream again.
Just open your heart and let freedom in.

MY TREASURE

It's hard when God shows me something I don't want to see—

Something that needs to change in my life immediately;
A truth I am not ready to hear;
A reality that, if I don't change, it will soon be here.

Then I remember these insights are a blessing to me.
They're words of discernment that are given freely.
So, I take this treasure with an open mind.
I'll put it to use while I still have time.

The treasure of wisdom can be immeasurable.
Only when applied does it become your treasure.

KEEP CALM

Keep calm, and always remember to put the armor of God on.
Don't ever leave your house unprepared.
Put on your shoes of hope to walk over despair.

Don't forget to put your socks of diligence on to cover your feet.
They'll help insulate you from life's disappointments so that you can continue to walk steadily.

Wrap yourself in faith to cover your skin, never letting the darkness of the world find its way in.

When the weight of the world makes you stumble and fall,
Ask yourself why you are carrying that burden at all.

Cover yourself in the knowledge that you have a companion who'll share the load,
Always faithful and present, loving you with nothing owed.

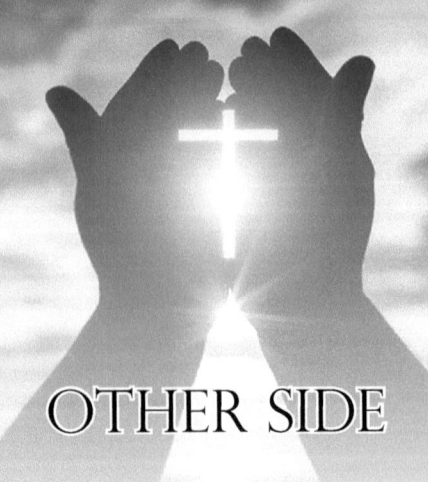

OTHER SIDE

Sometimes, the spirit doesn't rise as high.
It might be weighed down by the trials and tribulations of life.

Sometimes, the teardrops can't help but fall
Because there's no room internally to try to manage it all.

Sometimes, the hope is hard to create
When what's in front of you completely blocks your way.

Many times, those moments will turn out to be bittersweet.
I believe on the other side is where you'll find your testimony.

BREAKING UP

I've decided that it's time for us to split up.
You go your way because I've had enough.
I'm tired of looking at the same old stuff,
Because it won't change; so I'm calling your bluff.

If I stay, then I can never move forward.
I'll keep living what's already gone.
I'll never claim what's mine; I'll never learn how to move on.

So this is the last day that I'm going to live here.
I'm breaking up with my past so I can move in with my future.

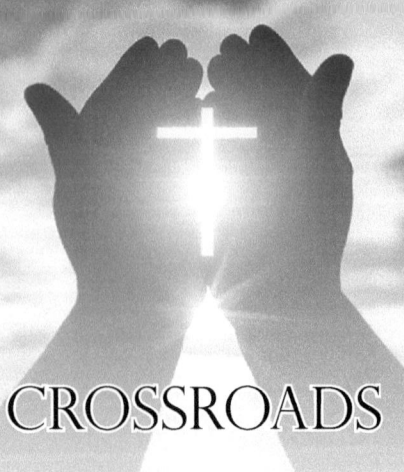

CROSSROADS

Lord, I stand at a crossroads
Where life and life meet,
Promising immediacy versus eternity,
Asking my heart to evaluate which one means more to me.

Worldly oppression and selective prosperity
Color the perceptions of what to believe,
Absolutely certainty with shame and guilt on display,
A perfect ingredient to push God's children away.

Still, I know better, as wisdom was planted in me,
Causing conflict between what my soul and eyes see,
For higher thoughts and higher ways are going on around me.
I pray for love and connection for all eternity,
So I guess the answer's right in front of me.

HEART

What has been planted in your heart today?
Is it a seed of bitterness and disappointment that just won't go away?
Is it the bloom of love or hope with anticipation of what's to come?
Is it the start of atrophy toward everyone?

Your heart helps more than blood flow through your veins.
A healthy heart will supply you the oxygen you need,
Feeding your soul, your cells, your physical body.

Just like your eyes, your heart can help you see.
Just like your feet and your hands, your heart can help you move purposefully.
When you fall down, your heart can be bruised,
Making you want to protect whom you show your heart to.

Your heart is a weapon against the things you hate,
Like oppression, poverty, starvation—the things that darken your way.
Hate, in this context, is not a bad thing,
For your heart needs to know the war that you are in.
It's the only thing that can fight the darkness that is trying to descend,
Using your heart as a weapon of love to let light in.

Your heart is the repository of all you need
To survive and thrive on your journey.
Feed your heart with faith and fuel from your soul.
Feed your soul with confidence that God is in control.

THE MOUNTAIN

The mountain appeared to block your view.
It created an obstacle you couldn't see around.
It created a challenge where blessings would be found,
Because the mountain wasn't built to stop you.
It was put in your path to show you what God can do.

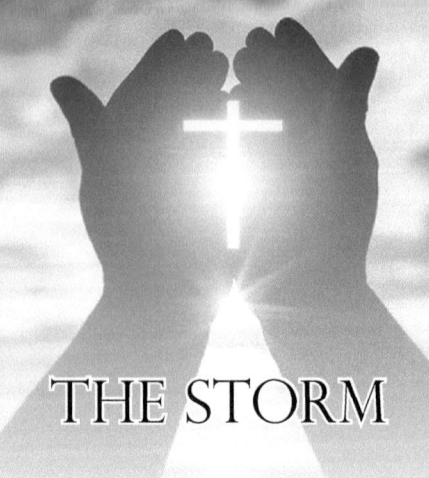

THE STORM

I was on a plane, and a storm was in our way.
The pilot told the flight attendants to sit, and that's when I started to pray.
We rocked from side to side, and the plane went up and down.
My stomach turned, my hands began to sweat, and I started to pray aloud.
I was praying and praying with no relief, and the clouds were swirling around.
I wanted this storm to end, to be home and back on the ground.

Then I thought about the storms in our lives,
Where the pilot tells us to sit because he is on our side,
Where we toss around with no relief in sight,
Where we hope we land and make it through this dark place in our life.

Well, the pilot knows just where he's going, and we will finally make it through.
We just have to hold fast, sit in faith, and trust our pilot, God, knows what he's doing.

TRUST

Sometimes, it's hard to leap when you don't see the other side.
It's hard to trust and believe God is working in your life.

Sometimes, the counsel of others makes you doubt what you believe,
Makes you cling to what you know and only to what you see.

Sometimes, it's hard to listen and hear the words "I know,"
"The plans I have for you," "the path that you should go."

Those first steps are often the hardest, and doubt slows your feet
Like prison chains, holding you back from your destiny.

Break your doubt with the solvent of confidence,
Pouring your trust and faith over those things that hold you back.

With faith and trust residing in your life,
You'll learn to leap and soar in the assurance of the Most High.

MY TESTIMONY

I live a quite ordinary life.
I get up in the morning.
I come home in the evening.
I'm a mother and a wife.

I'm also someone who has seen what God can do
When darkness and depression take over you,
When confidence is dead and your soul has gone astray,
When life becomes colorless and you're living in the gray.

When hope becomes a fantasy,
Your world quite turned around,
No sense of direction or destination is to be found.

Then the seed of faith that I planted so long ago becomes deeply rooted
inside me, and slowly, it starts to grow.

With that growth come confidence and hope for beautiful things, not
possessions but the simple essence and qualities that a faithful life brings.

It doesn't get rid of my struggles, my pain, or all my fears,
Yet it gives a place to go and leave those burdens here.

My days are lighter, and my spirit sings with joy; my trust is rock-solid, rooted in the Lord.

I share my testimony because your story can be someone's food, letting them know they're not alone, and if you seek, you will find there's something waiting for you.

WHEN

When the changes of life show up in waves,
It makes the ground unstable, like you're living in a tsunami every day.

When the hurt and pain feel like a million tiny cuts,
When the wounds won't heal because new feelings of pain erupt,

When the light is blocked by the darkness and clouds overwhelm,
It makes it hard to understand what path you're really on.

Just maybe

The waves are meant to shape you on your path,
Taking you in a direction where growth and wisdom are yours to have.

The cuts are there to notify you of the pain.
When you recognize pain, it tells you something needs to change.

When the darkness appears, perhaps it's not your path.
Maybe you shouldn't move farther until you fellowship with the inner
light you have.

Darkness may mean you only rely on what you see.
Sometimes, your eyes are not your truth nor what you should believe.

And just maybe

It's a tough season, and you must pray and believe you will make it through—

That this life's journey holds so much more for you.

THE NUTRIENTS OF TROUBLE

Oh look, it seems like I'm getting more food—
New troubles and concerns for me to absorb.
While I could look at these things and wonder, *Why me?*
Instead, I wait with anticipation quite eagerly.
These situations provide me food;
New strength, wisdom, endurance, and knowledge are born.
So don't look at troubles as a bad thing;
Look at them like a long-awaited meal providing nutrients.

THIRSTY WILL

Some days, I feel dry,
Like all the nutrients have been sucked out of my life.
Just a little parched from sitting in the sun,
From standing still for a little too long,
I thirst for my destiny.
Yet I find I'm not moving my feet,
Only watching the things that flow by me.
It's hard to find the energy to move when I'm so thirsty,
Yet the nutrients I need are so far in front of me.
In some ways, it feels like a mirage,
But what it really is, is a destiny that is unfulfilled,
Telling me I need to turn my doubtful drought into a thirsty will.

FROM PAIN TO PROSPERITY

The pain brought me to my knees.
It was in that place I begged God to take it from me.
Pain's melody was so beautifully played,
Making my life cry tears of heartache every day.
Each tear fell like a beat of a drum.
Each breath became harder to draw on.
Each burden felt so heavy on my soul.
Each daylight birthed another day to endure.

The pain was my indicator that something was wrong.
If I were immune to pain, I might have missed what was going on.
Without the pain, I don't know if I would've ever sought prayer.
I don't know if I would have kept suffering alone, resting in my despair.
Without the pain, I would've never crawled to my secret place—
The place I go to fellowship—but in that moment, I was trying to hide away.

Instead of hiding, it became my refuge of peace,
Bathing me in healing, making me cry in relief,
Soothing my heart and making my shoulders light,
Healing my feet so I could carry on with life,
Clearing my vision, giving me so much clarity,
Helping me avoid pits and obstacles I never saw in front of me.

I never knew my pain could lead me to prayer, helping me find inner peace,
Bringing me closer to the light of the Lord, overpowering the darkness.
Instead of a place of doom, my pain turned out to be
The entry point of my life filled with prosperity.

WHAT I SEE

I'm so glad I'm not what I see.
If I were, I wouldn't accomplish anything.
If I were, no one would believe in me.
If I chose to look only at today, I might not see possibilities.

I'm so glad I'm not what I see.
If I were, my ego would be too big,
Thinking that I've accomplished what I've been given,
Or better yet, what I've earned for a living
Has been all my own and not God-given.

I'm so glad I'm not what I see.
If I were, I could not walk in faith.
If I were, I wouldn't know God's grace.
If I were, doubt would rule my life.

I pray to look beyond what I see
To use my spiritual eyes to guide me
To walk in faith and confidence every day
That the Lord will help show me my path and light my way.

DREAM

Dream a dream that's worth repeating.
Learn to dwell less on those things that are depleting.
Sing a song loudly of hope and faith.
Learn to mute the things that take hope and faith away.
Laugh in the face of all your fears.
Let new strength be born created by your tears.
Drown hate and apathy with a river of love.
Bury those things that manifest in darkness, and let them grow no more.
Wake up every morning to live out your dream.
Cherish the essence of life and all the richness it can bring.

EXCESS WEIGHT

I woke up one day and noticed I had gained a lot of weight;
It hurt to walk, and my shoulders felt so heavy.
It seemed like I overate on the things I saw,
Like heartache, pain, and everyday drama.

I had stopped shedding and letting go of these things.
I had started to dwell on *Why me?* and *Why is this happening?*
Instead of believing and holding on faithfully.

The first thing I let go of was the feeling of defeat.
All of a sudden, my shoulders weren't so heavy.
Then I removed the fears and all my doubts.
I replaced them with confidence that this will all work out.

Finally, I removed the shackles of pain that were holding me.
Slowly, I was moving around pain-free.
It felt so good to move around with those weights off me.

If I'm not careful and diligent, the weight will come back.
It's a weight I was never supposed to carry or have.
I have to keep remembering my trainer's word.
No burden or weight is too heavy for the Lord.

PLANTED

Imagine you're in a garden.
What type of soil would you be planted in?
Would it be rich with fertilizer for you to flourish,
Or would it lack nutrients, stunting your growth?
Would it be bountiful with water nourishing your roots,
Or dry and brittle with a drought surrounding you?
Would you bask in sunlight to light your way,
Or would it be darkness and dreary days?
Where you are planted will impact your seed.
Without nourishment, you can't become a tree.

MY SPIRITUAL SWORD

Today, I decided to use my spiritual sword,
The one that was gifted to me by the Lord.
I was told that it would help me decipher the truth.
It would help me stay on the narrow road and give me insight on what
I should do.
It's made to grow my faith and wisdom exponentially.
It tells me of the love that Christ has for me.
It's food for my mustard seed.
It's the daily bread and spiritual nourishment that I need.
It can change my thoughts and my ways.
It can guide me through the struggles I experience day after day.
It was freely given from the Most High.
It supplies everything I need to survive—
Not just survive but live in the confidence that God's Word gives.

RESILIENCE'S BIRTH

My tears start to fall.
I try to resist the internal turmoil.
It boils up, looking for release,
Leaving me cracked with broken pieces.
Still with the exhale, it leaves no relief,
Praying that the weight will depart from me.
Over time, the burden dissipates.
Left in its place is new strength.

GOD'S SILENCE

There are times where I think God is not listening.
I ask for help and pray for wisdom.
I wait for an answer to my prayer.
I ask God, after waiting, "Are you still there?"
I become disappointed and let down in the silence.
After a while, I start to wonder where God went;
Better yet, was he even there in the beginning?

I stop hoping and waiting to hear;
I move forward, believing God never heard my prayer.
I never stop to think maybe God is working on my behalf.
Maybe the silence is preparation for my blessings to come to pass.

Maybe it was never silence but a chance for me to know
God's answers are different from my own.

WRONG TURN

Have you ever thought you made a wrong turn—wrong road, wrong destination—on your life's quest?
You wish you had asked for directions, a map, or simply a GPS.

You don't know how you got there, or better yet, you do.
You wish you could retrace your steps and start your journey anew.

Going back to the place where you made a right but should have gone left,
There's really no point in rehashing those wrong steps.

Although you're in a place you don't want to be,
There are always maps, guidance, hard work, prayers, and expressed actions to change your journey.

UNCONDITIONAL LOVE

Sometimes, I have to truly remember the unconditional love Christ has
for me.
I have to remember I did nothing to earn it, yet it is given freely.
Sometimes, in the quiet moments, my eyes fill with tears
Just thinking about the pure love that Christ gives.

Then I take a moment and look through my eyes and see
That I don't always try to love others like Christ loves me.
I've been changed by human unkindness and atrocities.
My heart has been toughened by disappointments and failings.

I feel like a victim caught in world experiences,
Guarding my love with barbed wire and tall fences,
Letting a select few in, and none escaping me,
Basing my extension of love on whom I deem worthy.

Then I go back to thinking, *God saw the worth in me,*
Then extended his mercy and love so graciously.
I know I can never come close to the love that God gives,
But my life should be an example of sharing godly love as long as I live.

UNFAIR TRADE

There are times where I make an unfair trade.
I choose worry over peace,
Disappointment over hoping.
I give up confidence and choose to focus on just coping.
I let love diminish, and apathy takes its place.
I stop thinking about tomorrow and focus on yesterday.
I take in insomnia and give away a restful sleep.
I lose a positive outlook and find one that's pretty bleak.
In the end, these all come down to really unfair trades,
So I'll choose to hold on to the things of value and give the worthless
things away.

FORGETTING OR FORGIVING

There are times when I wonder, *Do we mix up the two?*
It seems like forgetting is what we're asked to do.

Forgetting means we should let go of what we've gone through.
Forgiving means we accept what occurred and choose to deliberately move on.

Sometimes, I hear the words, "Well, that was so long ago,"
Yet those things that happen in the past can affect future growth.

It's hard to move on when there is a lack of acknowledgment of accountability.
It seems like we're asked to forget, not forgive, because absolution is what we seek.

I guess in the end, what I'm saying is it's not up to the accused to choose the path.

It rests in the hands of those you hurt whether forgetting or forgiveness is yours to have.

MY STRESS

I realized one day when I was really stressed
It is a problem I give to myself.
I know life is hard with many challenges,
But the weight I give it is self-evaluated.
So I'm going to take away the weight
And lift myself up in confidence each and every day
That whatever challenges I may face,
I'll overcome them day by day.

I WONDER

I wonder, *If I lit a candle for every forgotten dream,*
Would a satellite image show the world on fire?
I wonder, *If I cried a tear for every missed opportunity,*
Would the land be buried underwater?
I wonder, *If I sighed with every show of hate,*
Would there be any air left to breathe?
I wonder, *If I carried others' burdens,*
Would I be completely buried?

The world is a heavy place, and for everything, the opposite can appear.

Don't forget that chasing dreams, grabbing opportunities, loving one another, and sharing of burdens is why we were placed here.

MY SPIRITUAL SURGERY

I was scheduled for surgery
To remove the pain within,
To clean out my heart of worry,
To give hope a place to begin.

I had a biopsy to understand if I had a malignant growth,
A heart tumor of unforgiveness,
And I stubbornly refused to let go.

I had an MRI to see how much stubborn pride lived in me—
If it blocked my heart from understanding how to look at things humbly.

Then, finally, they took a blood test to see if there was anything that
was missed.
I just didn't want to put my spiritual life at risk.

Each and every day, I have to self-assess
What will cause me turmoil and what gives spiritual rest,
For each and every day, I treat like a surgery,
Which can bring death or life to me.

AWAKE

When it's nothing but a bad dream,
You wake up to experience the same thing
Over and over again, living the same mistake,
Wishing you could change tomorrow by going back to yesterday.
Be careful, because that's the definition of *regret*—
Keeping you stuck in your past like it's your present.
Leave your bad dream and choose to stay awake,
Making a choice to live for today.

WHAT DO YOU DO?

What do you do when you see the people you love in pain?
Oh, how you wish you could shoulder it for them.
You want to take the worry from their eyes.
You wish you could replace it with laughter, instead of the tears they cry.
You wish your hope were a nourishing thing,
Something they could eat to shore up their faith.
You pray in the darkness for the light of relief.
Every day, you awake, expecting that it was a bad dream.
You cling to the chance for a miracle to arrive,
Praying that they get through this dark patch in their lives,
Not just survive but prosper with a heart of peace—
A stronger spirit and resolve based on what they've achieved.
While you can't shoulder their burdens, one thing that you can do
Is be there to encourage with love and help them make it through.

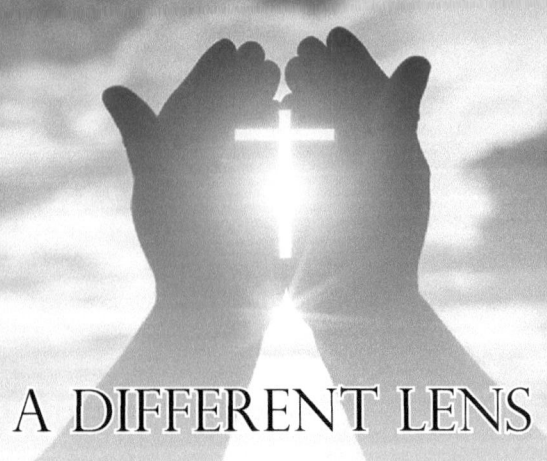

A DIFFERENT LENS

So I wear glasses to see.
Sometimes, I wish that life were a little more blurry
So I wouldn't have so much clarity
To see the darkness in front of me.

I think I'll start using different lenses.
I'll look for where I can find hope rather than despair.
I'll look for people who show me they care.

I'll look for joy in the midst of pain.
I'll search for connectivity to close the divide.
I'll seek truth and honesty instead of accepting lies.

I'll look for the light that resides in us all.
I'll stop believing that humanity has to fall.
It takes effort and work to look at things optimistically.
We need to seek and grow the things we want to continue to see.

BREATHE

Lately, I've found it takes a lot to breathe.
It's something you have to do consciously.
Life sends waves of things to make you feel like there's no air—
Obstacles, hurdles, barriers, suffering, and feelings of despair.

Just remember to take one breath at a time.
Remember to inhale and exhale, and you'll be fine.
Each inhale will build your strength to overcome.
Each exhale will expel the toxins of the situation.
Each deep breath will shore up your resolve.
Each gasp for air will show you, you can go on.

You were made with the power to breathe.
You are equipped to rise above those suffocating things.
Stand tall, rise up, and give yourself the time
To breathe through the situation one conscious breath at a time.

YOUR KEY

I was waiting for someone to free me,
But then I realized the only person who could release me was me.
Then I thought, *Dang, that's a shame.*
It seems I've gotten comfortable being confined by these chains.

I had started to realize that doubt was holding me down,
Wrapping itself around me, keeping me stuck in stagnant ground,
Hiding my path forward; so unsure of where was the road,
I feared taking a step, thinking of where I would go.

Then a voice said softly, "You hold the key—
The key to your path, your confidence, your freedom.
The path forward is the one you create,
Taking whatever determined steps day after day.

Don't be your own worst enemy, holding on to those suffocating things.
Be your biggest champion, speaking confidence that you can obtain
your dreams.
Be your biggest encourager; say you can overcome anything.
Use your key of hope and determination to find out what you truly can
obtain."

DREAM SEEDS

I had dreams in my heart that looked like seeds.
I put them in a drawer, hiding away hopeful things.
I think I realized in the drawer they would never grow
Without the exertion of effort and the sunlight of hope.
With my seeds hidden, they started to shrivel away,
Increasing my belief that they were never meant to be.
Seeds are meant to be planted, and then you'll see
That only then can your dreams come into your reality.

PLAN

I woke up with a plan today,
So I made myself a list.
I did nothing on that plan,
So my plan is now a wish.

THE BIRTH OF DESPAIR

Uncertainties, dark fumes fill the air,
Exhaling hope while I inhale despair.

Finding it hard to take in deep breaths,
My gasping and wails of crying are all that's left.

I sit in doom, waiting for the end to come.
The end marks the death of hope and the birth of pain
Buried deep in my soul, leaving me forever changed.

Still, I fight darkness, holding on to a beacon of light
Till that light is smothered and dies before my eyes.
So in the stillness of darkness, I wait to be free,
Begging that one day, despair will let go of me.

MY MOTHER'S MOTHER

My mother's mother wasn't free to love another.
I can still remember her face.
She taught me love, kindness, and grace.
We were truly blessed that she was once part of the human race.

Her frail, crooked hands hurt and throbbed every day.
Her walk was a shuffle; arthritis made her pay.
Still, she was my dream
That things didn't have to be like they seem.
She showed me how to believe.
She taught me how to achieve.
She gave me a reason to grieve.
She passed on her wisdom to me
So that I could live a life that's free—
Free of shackles and poverty,
Free to believe that it's all in me
To be whatever I want to be.

YOUR FUTURE

Don't put me away like I'm already gone.
Don't you dare act like I've already moved on,
'Cause if you're here, then I'm here, and I really want to stay.
Yesterday doesn't have to define you if you move forward with me.
Some things haven't been written because you're the author; it's really up to you.
Don't let others tell you that I'm gone or that we're through.
So we've had to adjust and self-correct, but that's part of the plan.
That new wisdom, new insight, new knowledge can make you a better person.
There are many paths in front of us that we can take.
Just remember that your tomorrow you can choose today.

TAKE A LOOK

Take a look in the mirror, and remember this face.
It's the one staring back at you that you see every day.
Get familiar with the imperfections that it wears.
Get up close and look deeply to see what's there.
Remember you are unique, wonderfully and fearfully made.
No diamond or jewel is the same in the human race.
Things of extreme value hold a rarity and are hard to find,
So when you stare at your unique eyes, your smile, your spirit, keep those things in mind.

"HELLO" TO "I DO"

Help me get from "hello" to "I do."
Help me focus on the right steps, the right clues.
Help me open my heart and be vulnerable.
Give me hope and signs to hold on to.
I know that you will lead me and my heart on this path.
I know that I'm covered and my loneliness won't last.
I know there's a partner and a godly man I'll find.
I'll trust you and speak a confident truth in my life
That you have someone whom you've designed for me;
That we are on the same path, the same journey;
That our roads will cross. Just trust and believe.
I'm highly favored, a child whose Father is a King.

HELLO

I'm starting to sense some doubt.
It's been a little while since we've hung out.
You seem to shy away whenever I'm around,
Not acknowledging my presence when I'm surrounding you.
Instead, you do the things that make it hard for me to come back,
Like devaluing who you are and listening to self-doubt.
Please don't let me go, because I'm important to you.
If you keep me, we can make it through
Disappointments, heartache, and uncertainties.
All I ask is that you cling and don't let go of me.

Forever yours,
Self-Love

MY INSTINCT

You know, when I'm scared, I turn to God in prayer.
It's like my survival instinct kicks in and I turn to the one whom I believe in.
Sure, when little things happen in my life,
I try to cope and just make it by.
But when I'm frightened deep in my core,
I don't play around; I go right to the Lord.
Think about a moment when your back was against the wall,
Where you had nowhere to turn; you saw your demise or fall.
Whom in that moment did you call?
I think that your instinct knows and wouldn't lie.
It goes to the Lord, whom internally you trust to help you survive.
It is in that moment that a thought enters my soul:
God is not just for emergencies but a place to daily go.
He is daily nourishment that gives peace to my soul.
It is when I rest in God's promises that I learn to be,
Not overcome by fear, pain, hurt, or anxiety.
And through daily fellowship, it builds strength in me.
So I have learned from my instinct what I thought I already knew:
That God is the truth, the light, and where my soul is renewed.

BUMPY RIDE

Life is a bumpy ride.
If it was smooth sailing, what would it generate?
I'm sure that this is something that could be up for debate.
If life was not complicated and was quite easy,
Would it build character, strength, faith, and vulnerability?
Look back, and think about what you might not have accomplished in your journey.
Think about those dark times in your life and the things you had to fight.
Would you have ever known what it feels like without darkness—how it is to live in the light?
In those times, don't reflect on the bumpy ride.
Focus, and stay expectant on what you will obtain on the other side.

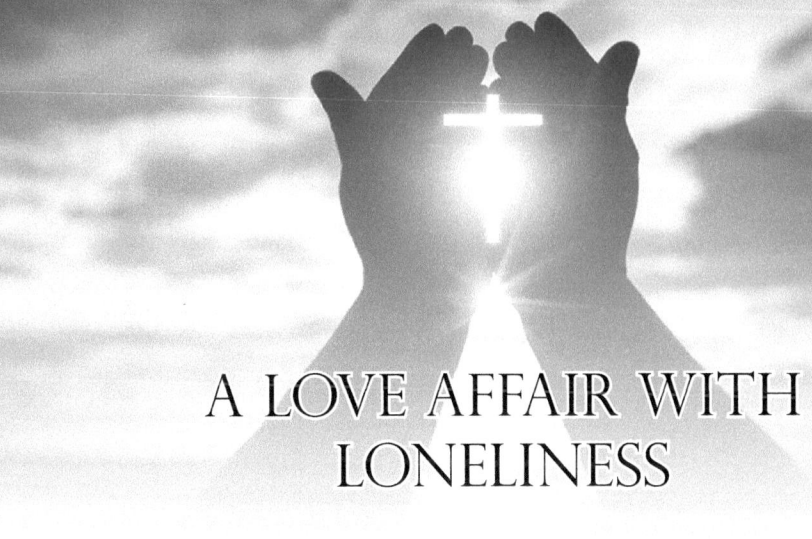

A LOVE AFFAIR WITH LONELINESS

I think it's time for us to dance,
To come together for a little romance—
Perhaps a night that you'll remember,
An evening under the moonlight, sharing dinner;
Or an evening watching TV, just you and me.
There's no need for any other company.
I'm your rock, your ace, your one in the hole.
I'll always return, especially when the nights get cold.
I'm dependable, reliable; no need to call on me.
Even though I hate crowds, I can show up there too, eventually.
There's no place for you that I cannot be.
Sometimes, you would be so surprised where you can find me.
The only time I choose to not return to at all
Is when you make a connection with vulnerability and let your walls fall.
Behind those walls is a beautiful person the world needs to see.
It's your connection with others; in that place, you won't find me.

YEARNING IN THE MUCK

Yearning in the muck,
Desire is stagnant,
Paralysis while life moves.
How do I change
My cast-down eyes?
The truth of me too hard to bear,
The potential doesn't taste palatable;
Instead, the potential tastes bitter.
The desire tastes salty
From my tears of despair.
The yearning smells sour
From the length of time it's sat here.
My destiny remains make-believe
Because it's a dream where I have yet to wake up and see it.

DYING IN THE SUN

The darkness burns within
Blanketed by the isolation of loneliness,
Securing its togetherness.

The empty feelings aside,
The desire that died
Thirsty for lust,
The desert runs dry,
Leaving starvation.

The words that choke
Stuck in your throat,
Their abundance leads to death,
Suffocating on all that's unsaid.

The tears flow freely,
Bathing the ground in minerals that provide no nourishment,
Leaving the seed unfertilized
With seeds that go dormant,
With roots left unplanted
To die in the sun.

I'm broke but not broken.
I'm hurt but not damaged.
I'm down but not hopeless.
While my smiles are few,
My soul is peacefully renewed.

PERSPECTIVE

Perspective—
Two sides of the same coin.
Choose the lens that you look through—
Clear, faint, pure, or tainted.
The situation gets what you give it.

FAVOR

While I sit
Contemplating
What you've done for me,
I know you have always looked out for me.

God kept me
And he saved me time and time again.
His grace for me is amazing;
Favor I truly have.

God—he loves me.
He tells me so; he whispers my sweet name
(Latisha).

God—he holds me, my life complete,
My world forever changed
(I'm yours).

Waves have rocked me.
Stones have hurt me.
People come, and people go; some desert me.
Then you hold my hand; then I know where I am.
It's in your arms, which I call *home*.
You stay with me, though I am often weak.

I have favor—
So much favor.
God turns everything into favor.
You can't hurt me;
It turns into strength.

It's because the Lord is always with me.

I'M NOT SAD

Jesus keeps me
And holds me, and my dark is made to light.
He exposes emotion; my sins are made plain.
No hiding nor denying, his love makes you change.

Buried deep, there's a need for your soul to be whole.
"Intercede on our behalf,
The lover of our soul."

Give the pain to God.
He knows what to do.
He makes it lighter for you.

I'm not sad.

Every day, there's a way for the world to be cold,
Touching you with pain; that's hard to endure.
Run this race with your head pointed toward the sky.
Though you may stumble and fall, you know where your strength lies.

God's there for you.
God will see you through.
Your burden is not yours;
Give it over to the Lord.

I'm not sad.

Hold your hand to the sky; let your life give him praise.
Let him know that the world won't crush you today,
For you draw your strength from an endless supply.
If you believe in the Lord, you know where your grace lies.

God's there for you.
God will see you through.
Your burden is not yours;
Give it over to the Lord.

I'm not sad.

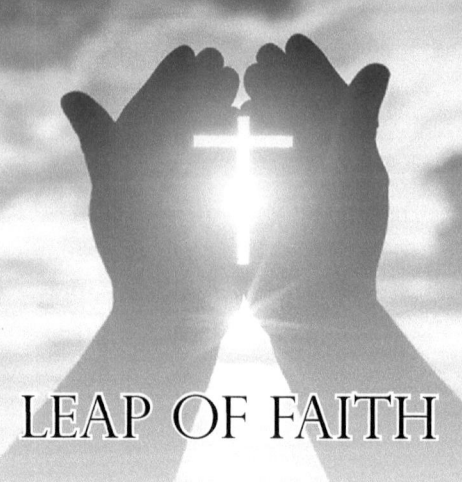

LEAP OF FAITH

Sometimes, the truth may seem hard to bear,
The mountain too steep to climb.
The way that you eat an elephant
Is take one bite at a time.

Sometimes, the world may seem difficult.
They stand in front of you.
Just take a leap and jump over
Those who stand in front of you.

Sometimes, the world may seem unfair,
The burden too much to bear.
The way that you walk one thousand miles
Is each step will get you there.

Sometimes, the world may not help you,
Doors closing every day.
The way that you create opportunities
Is to look a different way.

Just take a leap and jump over
What stands in front of you.
Just take a step and come over;
Your barriers don't own you.

Just take a leap and believe in faith.
Your heart will see you through.
Just take a step and jump off the ledge;
The path's in front of you.

THE END

The end is only the beginning.
It is there that the Lord said, "It is finished."
So leave whatever you are suffering there.
Drop it in the Lord's hand in prayer.
It is finished.
It is gone.
It has no power over you.
Its grip has loosened, and you can start to recover from what you went
through.
You can let the wound breathe and become a scar,
For such scars are a testament of your mighty power.

And through wounds, scars, and battles you have fought,
Through tears, wails, and darkness surrounding you,
You sought the light, or it sought you.
Either way, remember these words:
It is the end, and it is finished.

Now, seek the nourishment of your truth to be replenished.
You are mighty; you are strong; your existence is not by chance.
You were created for this time and circumstance.

You are loved even when you don't believe
That someone would love the likes of thee.

Make this ending a final note.
Now, begin a melody to journey on your new road.

PEDOMETER

So I started to wear a pedometer the other day.
It helped me count the amount of steps I take.

I wish I could count the steps I take in my spiritual journey
To know if I am making progress in my faith.

THE CALAMITY OF CONFORMITY

I move in the direction of the wind,
Swaying in sync, perfectly fitting in.
I see no ripples in the waves,
No one clapping offbeat in our society.
We all walk at the same pace,
Agreeing that our destination is this way.
We don't question or challenge openly.
We bottle and dismiss any uncertainty.
We focus on the future and the steps we must take.
Linking hands and voices, we are strongly united.
We are marching, but the road comes to a stop.
We are perplexed because this path was clearly marked.
We are dumbfounded because we all had agreed.
There is no way we went the wrong way on the journey.
How could we have gone the wrong way?
We all had agreed on our destiny.
No one stopped to ask if this was right.
No one disagreed or put up a fight.
Marching ahead clearly, yet blindly,
We created victims of conformity.

MAYDAY

I wonder if we recognize the trouble we are in,
The way we are divided as a nation letting the ugliness settle in.
Mayday is a term meaning "a cry for help."
It's when you don't know how to fix it or really help yourself.

It's a scream of release, hoping that your plea is heard.
It's a search for hope and love to be released into the world.
It's begging that comes deep from your soul,
Wanting no longer for the world to be divided but for it to become whole.

It's okay to scream, "Mayday!" and plead for a rescue.
It's okay to wish that we could look into each other's eyes and start fresh,
hopeful and renewed.
I don't claim to have the answer to what we've become.
I just know the path has to change from the journey that we are on.

THE CONSTRUCTION
OF INEQUALITY

The lack of smoothness, irregularity on the surface, goes very deep.
It starts at the core of who we are and what we believe.
It's built layer by layer with generational upbringing
Supported by cracks of separation, lacking foundational understanding.

It's a mix of ingredients that further solidify the structure—
Education, health care, careers, and economic wealth—
Constructed layer by layer until inequality supports itself.
A structure without intervention will continue to remain strong
Built on the sturdy backs of those long gone.

STAND

The time to stand is now.
We shouldn't escape to the moral high ground.
Eventually, there'll be nowhere to go.
By not standing, we've polluted our world.

It's time to stand in the divide,
To reach out and touch other lives,
To stretch beyond our comfortable space,
To look in the face at what separates us and say,
"You don't belong here."

Stand in the face of hate,
Coating it in love to deplete its strength.
Weaken and exposed, it's a place that love can grow.

Stand and see
That we are more alike than we believe,
That our differences create strength,
That our individual paths intersect,
Connecting us to a stronger place
That only together will we experience.

DYING VIRUSES (GOTTA LOVE THE NAME, RIGHT?)

There are viruses dying too quickly.
We take medicine to kill them constantly.
They have a prescription that's usually fairly cheap.
Most people give the cure away freely.
Those who try to feed them are sometimes looked at skeptically.

There, the types of viruses I wish would take hold
Spread like wildfire or just like the common cold,
Where they catch on fire or you could breathe them in every day,
Making a way for these viruses to go viral again.

Too bad they're not easily spread.
Most of the time, they're starving and never fed.
I wish they were given away like candy
To the point that we all had rotten teeth
Because we eat their sweetness constantly.

Kindness is renewable if we give it away.
Empathy is sustainable if we use it every day.
Love is abundant if we grow it bountifully.

Trust is essential if we feed it constantly.
Faith can begin with just a mustard seed.
Committed to spreading them faithfully,
Humanity will thrive if we spread these viruses freely.

ARMOR

I see so much armor as I walk through everyday life—
So many helmets hiding what's in the mind,
So many breastplates making the heart hard to find,
Gauntlets hiding a helping hand,
Making sure to not share beliefs with one's fellow man.

Protection is a double-edged sword.
Preservation of oneself, losing the strength of vulnerability,
Means that the armor inflicts less intimacy,

Causing a thickness of skin that's hard to break,
Leaving humanity as a casualty in its wake.

HOPE AND RESILIENCE

Side by side, they stand together,
Inseparable through disappointment and pain,
Leaning on each other time and time again.

Resilience says, "Defeat won't win.
It wants you to stay down there.
It wants you to pretend
That there is no other place you can go.
There is no other solution; defeat is all you'll know."

Hope is saying, "I really do believe
If we hang together, all things we can achieve.
I won't give up on you if you don't give up on me.
I see a vision of the future, and I know, if you stand with me,
That our future will come to pass, that our present will no longer be.

Pick me up whenever I stumble and fall.
Give me assurance to remember that there is no failure at all—
Only refinements until it comes to pass
Each lesson learned gives new information to grasp."

Resilience needing a seed to begin—
A seed of hope that lets a new future in.
No matter the circumstance or what's in front of you,
Carry these two things with faith, and all things are possible.

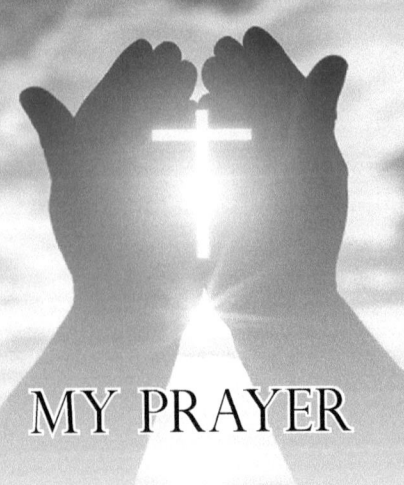

MY PRAYER

I pray for hope across our lands.
I pray for a future for all our children.
I pray for the generations we can't see
That we leave them an inheritance of world peace.
I pray that the decisions we make today
Will create prosperity for families.
I pray that no matter how bleak the world may seem,
We stoke the flame of love and hope in our communities.
I pray for a desire and hunger in man
To be servant leaders across our lands.

MY CANVAS

In the face of another year,
I recognize how far I have come,
Finally realizing that it's truly a journey I'm on.
Some moments are lovely, while others are not so pretty.
Still, in its collectiveness, I gasp at its beauty.

I reflect on my canvas and realize a few truths:
Some friends are forever, while others flutter through.
Pain can be the entrance to your prosperity and where your faith is
renewed.
Your children's eyes give you clarity of what you're fighting for.

Doubt hindered my canvas, and confidence helped me explore,
Showing me I can stretch, learn, and obtain so much more—
More colors, more lines and shades on my canvas—
That I'm not the observer but I am the artist.

So I guess what I'm saying is I have more painting to do—
That my canvas, while definitely started, is not yet final.

LABOR OF LOVE

My labor of love wasn't a labor of love until it came to pass.
Before that, it was only really known as a pain in my a**.
Now, I can finally look back at it nostalgically,
Smiling at the long nights and the lack of sleep,
Crying tears of joy instead of tears of frustration,
No longer holding doubt but holding my creation.

I feel like the accomplishment is really the dream,
Yet it's full circle, because the dream came before anything.
I'm so happy I didn't throw it away and I planted the seed.
I stuck with it, helping it grow into something.

The love wasn't born because it bore fruit;
The love was born as I looked back at my labor and where I made it to.

AFTERWORD

Thank you. I truly appreciate your support and, most important, your allowing me to share myself with you in a way that we rarely get to see one another. As I read some of the words I've written, I remember feeling the tears fall in my despair. I remember the joy and laughter when I captured hope developing in my life. These words reflect my inner struggles and life achievements. This book is my vulnerability on paper; it shares part of me rarely witnessed and definitely not talked about. I left the door open, and you came in to sit with me.

Sharing of ourselves is truly how we connect with the world; thank you for taking the time to read this. I hope you enjoyed the canvas I've created, and I would love to hear from you as you walk your own journey. Be blessed.